Counting Survivors

Also by Walter McDonald

Poetry Chapbooks

Splitting Wood for Winter, 1988
Working Against Time, 1981
One Thing Leads to Another, 1978

Poetry

Where Skies Are Not Cloudy, 1993
All That Matters: The Texas Plains in Photographs and Poems, 1992
The Digs in Escondido Canyon, 1991
Night Landings, 1989
A Band of Brothers: Stories from Vietnam, 1989
After the Noise of Saigon, 1988
Rafting the Brazos, 1988
The Flying Dutchman, 1987
Witching on Hardscrabble, 1985
Burning the Fence, 1981
Anything, Anything, 1980
Caliban in Blue, 1976

Fiction

A Band of Brothers: Stories from Vietnam, 1989

Counting Survivors

Walter McDonald

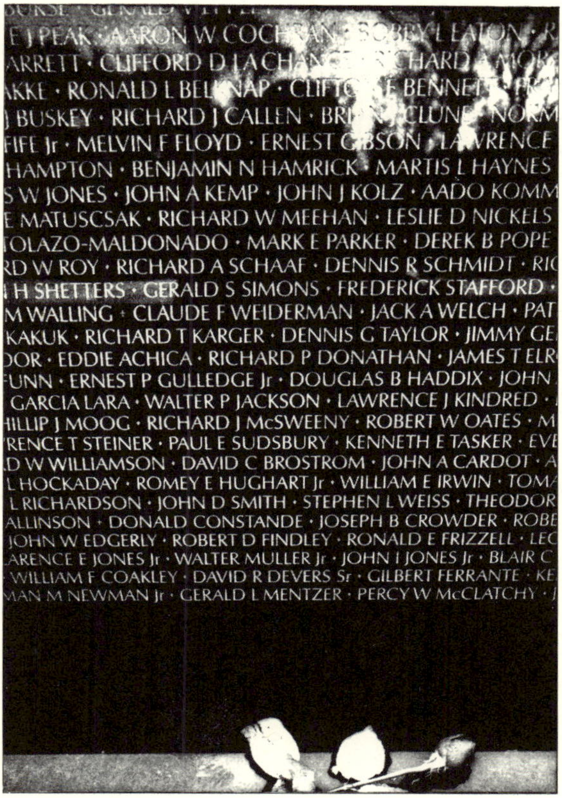

University of Pittsburgh Press
Pittsburgh • London

The publication of this book is supported by grants from the National Endowment for the Arts in Washington, D.C., a Federal agency, and the Pennsylvania Council on the Arts.

Published by the University of Pittsburgh Press, Pittsburgh, Pa. 15260

Manufactured in the United States of America

Printed on acid-free paper

Library of Congress Cataloging-in-Publication Data

McDonald, Walter.
Counting Survivors/ Walter McDonald
p. cm. —(Pitt Poetry Series)
ISBN 0-8229-3874-X (cl.).—ISBN 0-8229-5555-5 (pbk.)
I. Title. II. Series.
PS3563.A2914C68 1995 93-43044
811'.54—dc20 CIP

A CIP catalogue record for this book is available from the British Library.
Eurospan, London

Acknowledgments are located on page 81.

Book Design: Frank Lehner

For Jillian, David, Michael, and Jessica

Contents

I. Heirlooms

II. My Brother and the Golden Gloves

III. Roll Call

I. Heirlooms

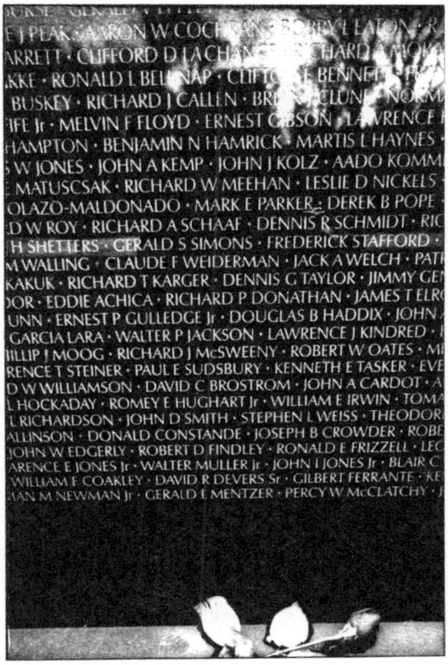

AARON W COCH
CLIFFORD D LACH
RONALD L BEL NAP
RICHARD J CALLEN
MELVIN F FLOYD · ERNEST G BSON
HAMPTON · BENJAMIN N HAMRICK · MARTIS L HAYNES
W JONES · JOHN A KEMP · JOHN J KOLZ · AADO KOMM
MATUSCSAK · RICHARD W MEEHAN · LESLIE D NICKELS
OLAZO-MALDONADO · MARK E PARKER · DEREK B POPE
D W ROY · RICHARD A SCHAAF · DENNIS R SCHMIDT
H SHETTERS · GERALD S SIMONS · FREDERICK STAFFORD
M WALLING · CLAUDE F WEIDERMAN · JACK A WELCH
KAKUK · RICHARD T KARGER · DENNIS G TAYLOR · JIMMY GE
OR · EDDIE ACHICA · RICHARD P DONATHAN · JAMES T ELR
UNN · ERNEST P GULLEDGE Jr · DOUGLAS B HADDIX · JOHN
GARCIA LARA · WALTER P JACKSON · LAWRENCE J KINDRED
HILLIP J MOOG · RICHARD J McSWEENY · ROBERT W OATES
RENCE T STEINER · PAUL E SUDSBURY · KENNETH E TASKER
D W WILLIAMSON · DAVID C BROSTROM · JOHN A CARDOT
L HOCKADAY · ROMEY E HUGHART Jr · WILLIAM E IRWIN
L RICHARDSON · JOHN D SMITH · STEPHEN L WEISS · THEODOR
ALLINSON · DONALD CONSTANDE · JOSEPH B CROWDER
JOHN W EDGERLY · ROBERT D FINDLEY · RONALD E FRIZZELL
ARENCE E JONES Jr · WALTER MULLER Jr · JOHN I JONES Jr · BLAIR C
WILLIAM F COAKLEY · DAVID R DEVERS Sr · GILBERT FERRANTE
MAN M NEWMAN Jr · GERALD L MENTZER · PERCY W McCLATCHY

After the Fall of Saigon

A mad man aging hard can't fight a war
forever. Think pity and the mind turns cold.
He still sees children and old men

ragged and golden, crawling the base dump
for scraps of food at sundown.
Years after Saigon, he's like a wall:

lets no one know him, but his name.
Stone-faced, he tries to wish it all away,
a harmless Buddha with a green patina,

envies the lucky ones who didn't go.
Even good booze can't burn the fungus out,
down where it doesn't show,

the mind's own groin. He takes another shot
to hold him till it's dark, but after that,
they're back.

Wishing for More than Thunder

Mirages hover like angels fanning the fields.
We see them in summer, a shimmer of wings.
Our stubborn steers ignore them, wading dry acres.
They hook their horns in invisible robes,

shaking their heads to graze. For them
the sky is falling, the grass is manna.
Having lost all hope when they entered
the round corral as calves, they stuff themselves

even in drought, as if all pastures
on the plains are theirs. They never wonder
if God's in His heaven. Stubble is fodder enough,
alfalfa paradise. Watching steers graze

in a lake of shimmering light, seeing angels
fanning themselves, we wonder if even they
could make it rain, how many spin on a windmill,
how many squeezed would make a decent cloud.

Harvest

No dogcatchers ride by, only cars
with pets like rejected hearts. Our stock tank
rescues dogs abandoned by cars with city tags.

Dogs starve if they aren't born hungry for blood,
part wolf, or cute as Disney dogs some farmer's daughter
begs him to adopt. Stray cats survive on mice and birds,

prowling somebody's barn. Stiff winds spread fires
to fields where pheasants risk the rattlers.
The sun leads cows to pasture, time for windmills

to spin their rapture, turning grass to milk.
Sometimes I squeeze a squirt to a row of cats
waiting with mouths wide with fangs. The farm

is harvest all year long. At night, rattlers
that survive the fires move rippling over rows,
and silent barn owls dive to pluck their staring eyes.

For Friends Missing in Action

Near the coast in snow,
we marched to the flight line,
swinging our arms in formation.
Old pilots huddled in hangers,

watching us shiver in flight suits.
Four hours of cockpit time,
staring at dials and switches,
hoping to solo. We sat in jets

we would know before long
blindfolded, cleared to take off
even in weather like that,
climbing through clouds to the sun.

We studied gauges and codes
like prayer beads, believing
nothing that big could kill us,
those wings would hold us up.

The Gleam of Silver Wings

After Darren's jet fell spinning
out of the Asian sky,
I learned the myth of perfect flight,

all of us Icarus, birds of a feather,
accident-prone ground pounders
riding throttled fire.

I had seen airplanes in movies
tumbling and spouting smoke
and flames from under,

but not real flesh, like Darren,
the first I knew overseas
who vanished

out of blue skies far from home,
no parachute open,
ten thousand pounds of thrust

and one of us reduced
to this, a silver matchstick
tossed indifferently away.

What If I Didn't Die Outside Saigon

So what do you want? he growled inside the chopper,
strapping me roughly to the stretcher
as if I were already dead. "Jesus," I swore,
delirious with pain, touching the hot mush of my legs.
"To see my wife. Go home, play with my kids,

help them grow up. You know." His camouflaged face
was granite, a colonel or sergeant who'd seen it all.
He wore a parka in the rain, a stubby stale cigar
bit tight between his teeth, a nicked machete
like a scythe strapped to his back. He raised a fist

and held the chopper. He wore a gold wrist watch
with a bold sweep-second hand. The pilot glanced back,
stared, and looked away. Bored, the old man asked,
Then what? his cigar bobbing. I swallowed morphine
and choked, "More time. To think, plant trees,

teach my kids to fish and catch a ball."
Yeah? he said, sucking the cigar, thinner
than he seemed at first. Through a torrent of rain,
I saw the jungle closing over me like night.
"And travel," I said, desperate, "to see the world.

That's it, safe trips with loved ones. Long years
to do whatever. Make something of my life. Make love,
not war." I couldn't believe it, wise-cracking clichés,
about to die. He didn't smile, but nodded. *So?*
What then? "What then? Listen, that's enough,

isn't that enough?" His cigar puffed
into flame, he sucked and blew four perfect rings
which floated through the door and suddenly
dissolved. Without a word, he leaned and touched
my bloody stumps, unbuckled the stretcher straps

and tore the *Killed-in-Action* tag from my chest.
And I sat up today in bed, stiff-legged, out of breath,
an old man with a room of pictures of children
who've moved away, and a woman a little like my wife
but twice her age, still sleeping in my bed.

Heirlooms

We're down to an anvil and conch,
sea shell and useless steel,
not much from four hard years
of war. Mother's grandmother

blew this shell like a horn,
one steady roar to warn
of soldiers scouring Alabama pines,
two blasts to bring him back.

Feel the smooth, curved shell,
taste the dust of the mouth hole.
Touch the knobs like knuckles,
the wavy edges chipped

before we were born. Rub the nicked,
smooth steel of the anvil.
Grandfather felt the smithy's blast,
watched his father pound red iron

until the muscles bulged,
about to burst. Grandfather touched
those fists, the massive biceps.
Feel the pink bowl of the shell,

slide your hand through the spiral
back to the days of Lincoln,
imagine owning ten burned acres
and a leg a Minié ball took off.

Sniff the Alabama pine,
a thousand miles of powder.
Hold it close and hear an ocean
roll near Mobile, blow it long,

now rapid puffs like a hoot owl—
listen to the ringing steel
on the anvil, the clang of hammers
pounding iron to plows.

Teaching Our Sons Old Chores

Easy, I tell our sons. They tempt our bulls
by offering themselves, vaulting over
and choking on dust and laughter. My father
would have jabbed his thumb in their ribs

and scoffed—*Think of those bulls as storks,*
their scrotums bundles swaying a range of calves.
My brother and I tormented bulls for years.
Our father made us clean the corral with brooms.

Now, our boys rake the same corral, dust devils
swirling. At dusk, huddled with coffee cups,
I toss a final log on the fire. Out come
the same tall tales like family albums,

nothing but stars and a moon to guide us
on geldings we raised ourselves.
Sparks disappear into skies so wide
they're ours, these endless plains our home.

Regular Programming on the Eve of War

And here we are again, back from Africa
on the trade winds. What a lark,
what a cunning little globe to trot

on the Discovery channel. We walk these plains
laid out by thousands of years of drought.
What holds us here comes back, high overhead

and burning. How many watched this sun
on landlocked prairies before us, hands up
like shields, squinting without a prayer

at black wings wheeling. Tonight on TV we'll buy
Tahiti with our eyes and snorkel coral reefs,
explore steel hulls with angel fish, sky dive

off Maui, relive an almost forgotten war
between newscasts from the Persian Gulf.
But now we wait outside together, staring

at flat land wide as our eyes can see,
the words we mumble our only prayer,
our only hope for peace.

War in the Persian Gulf

Someone I flew with sailed to the Persian Gulf
decades ago, a cadet we called Al, like others
from Colombia, Vietnam, exotic countries
far away on maps. Al was a swarthy, quiet Iraqi
with straight teeth, a handsome smile, cleft chin
and wide eyebrows. We teased that he kept harems
of veiled wives. Under his jaunty flight cap,

Al wasn't the first to solo, but the best.
His T-Scores proved it. His instructor
posted them at dawn to taunt us. We shouldered
parachutes and swaggered to the flight line
out of breath with boasts, spoiling for dog fights
over Georgia pines. Who ever met such friends,
men we would die for. Where is he now,

a general? Or sleepless in Baghdad,
worried about grandsons, still just a captain,
intractable, flying the slowest desk? Or shot down
years ago in Iran, bones in forgotten sands?
Or on alert in a French Mirage cockpit,
his handsome face lined, lips tight,
concealing his perfect teeth?

The Price They Paid for Range

Bone white caliche undercuts our dust.
Most trees dry up, stunted on starving roots.
To save imported stumps, we ditch the fields
with peat imported from swamps,
tamp bone meal into dirt for roses.
Cactus rode here as burrs with soldiers,
their Spanish ponies stumbling
under the sun, dumping knobs of seeds

from weed fields miles away.
Wind taught our fathers how to survive
so far from forests: build low and far apart
and ration water. Let stallions and cattle
be enough, rough bunks and windmills
the way to pray, cow chips for fire, cactus
and rattlers the price they paid for range
and a thousand miles of stars.

Out of the Stone They Come

My son hung a framed painting
on his wall. Head down, a man my age
leans on black granite. A soldier
holds out a ghostly hand to touch him.

Others beyond the wall look out,
young as my son in their helmets.
Out of the stone they've come
with incredibly young arms

because he's here, head bowed,
surviving. They don't seem to envy
his graying hair, black attaché case
or vest. He knows their names

and leans alone in sunlight.
Beside this frame in smaller frames
are shots of my boy's own friends
who'd never gone to war

until the Persian Gulf. One night,
we parked in blowing snow
and hunched a half mile slowly
to the wall, not talking about a war

he can't recall. While I looked for names
he waited, a soldier as old as those.
I rubbed my fingers on the words,
black granite cold as a mirror.

I saw my son's own image in the stone
but found no other face,
only a wide black wall
and names, names blurring together.

II. My Brother and the Golden Gloves

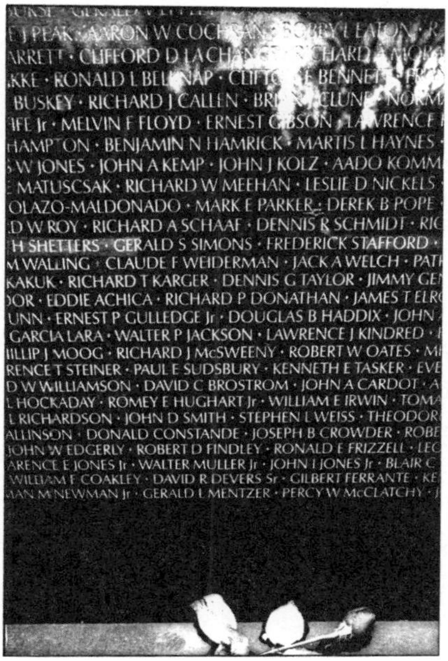

Life with Father

Sunday meant sleeping in,
time to pull another quilt
and hide from whiskey
in our daddy's snoring.

Only the Sunday funnies saved us
after last night's raving,
proof there was a demon.
Under covers we traded peeks

at Maggie giving Jiggs
the devil, Dagwood
bumbling about insanely sober,
tiny Wash Tubbs with twins

he doted over. At dawn
we folded the quilts
and funnies, crept softly
through our chores

as if in church,
soothing the fi-foe-fum
of his slumber, fearing
the thrum of his boots

descending the heavy
stalk of his stupor,
fierce when he found
his dreamed gold gone.

Boys with Chihuahua Dogs

Chihuahuas the size of mice
chased cicadas in our backyard
under willows they entered
like doorways draped with streamers.

We argued what they'd do if they caught one,
yip-yipping and leaping, tumbling
and running, clumsy as rocker horses.
Dogs we wore in our pockets

kept us in trouble at church,
Sunday school no home for creatures
hopeless, without souls. Once
they scampered like devils down aisles

while the pastor convinced us all
we were starving for mercy, choking back laughter,
dying for benediction. Our father,
who was in trouble with the board of deacons,

left us alone with our dogs
and conscience, preaching a gospel
to creatures small enough
to enter the kingdom of pockets.

Hairless like Mary's lamb after shearing,
they followed us often to school
and on bicycle errands for parents.
What can you say about dogs

too dumb to read stop signs,
too slow for cars in a speed zone,
too small for a shoebox,
too hopeless for a cross.

Digging in a Footlocker

Crouched before dismantled guns,
we found war souvenirs
our uncle padlocked in the attic,
a brittle latch easily pried off.

Stiff uniforms on top, snapshots
of soldiers young as our cousins,
a velvet box of medals
as if he fought all battles

in World War II. Bayonets, machetes,
a folded flag, two hand grenades
with missing pins. We picked up teeth
like pennies, loose, as if tossed in,

a piece of something dark and waxy
like a fig, curved like a question mark,
a human ear. We touched dried pieces
of cloth stuck to curved bones

and held them up to the light,
turning them over and over, wondering
how did uncles learn to kill,
what would happen when we grew up.

Seconds of Free-Fall and Chaos

My bored brother dragged me
away from Kiddie Land, shoved me
roughly to the adult ticket booth,
the line dividing me from men.

Thrilled by tickets snaking from his fist,
I entered the kingdom of risks—
the Hammer and Zipper, the roller coaster.
I flinched when the Hammer

slammed down, when the Zipper toppled
and flipped us. I held the bar
in a car jerked up a track
and watched tree tops and tents

fall away. My brother leaned close
and hissed how many fell
from these seats last year, flung out
over screaming mothers. He raised both hands

and made me, the crossbar loose on my lap.
Older boys tossed their hair
and laughed, the heads of girls
snug in their elbows.

Our car crawled on cables
grinding like bicycle chains
about to break, all rides of childhood
behind me, my arms high in surrender,

my skull wobbling
through tight turns, mashed down
like being born again to lights
and dazzling screams.

Buzzards and Uncle Douglas

Uncle Douglas taught his dogs to chase off
buzzards in the sky. He cursed their black apparel,
their bowed necks praying for the dead.
He wanted them starved above his dying trees.
Saplings died faster than he could haul them off,

nothing but lumber in his heart after Aunt Wanda died.
Douglas was a pharaoh of dying aspens, without a son.
Fungus killed all aspens on his farm, nothing to do
but cut them. He dropped his chain saw down
and stacked them, his skies haunted by a slow

whirlpool of wings. The old man loved those dogs
but never let strangers see him pet them,
never mind the moon, the nights we fished together,
the lake trout fighting for their lives. He taught me
the feel of mud underfoot, the way to cast

far out for lunkers. He hated anything that grieved
in public. From his woodlot we watched them
like a black mobile of mourners that never cared
for something while it lived. He cursed them all,
an old man lost in a forest who hated every day

he wasted while Aunt Wanda lived. Gruff, he taught me
to sit so still I heard stars burning. In August,
he harnessed the mule and let the road to the depot
keep us both from choking, holding me tight as a son
before my train pulled out.

Fame at Eleven

We pulled spring-loaded pins
and shot volleys over the heads
of rubber-covered posts. We played away
the buffalo coins of boyhood,

pushing the limit of balls,
the odds. Humped over,
we fumbled the button tits
of a machine, shoved pinballs

toward a bevy of pegs and clanging bells.
Guarding nothing but arc,
we cuffed the pinging machine
toward tilt, flipping steel balls

like defiance, slapping
to smash them back to the top
for a bonus. Butts dangling
from pouting lips, squinting,

we practiced macho poses in public,
aroused by the fame of older boys—
last month's amazing scores
chalked on a board above us.

My Brother and the Golden Gloves

My body knew the bold flurry of his fists.
Twelve and fifteen, we grew up brothers
in different worlds. He had scars
I knew made him a hero
though he hated fights,

the Golden Gloves our daddy's idea.
Boys pretending to be tough
stopped by, smoking their butts,
crushing them in our grass.
After they left, dried blood

stuck to his fists, the bridge of his nose.
Korea was almost lost when he enlisted.
I remember his fist in his hair
when he came home, as if he'd lost his comb.
He crushed cigarettes in ashtrays,

tried odd jobs and quit them.
I asked about the war, how many friends
he lost. He turned away as if to save me,
his right hand always a fist. Our father
gave him the car and sold the fatted calf

and gave him that to hold him.
I remember gravel pinging
the family sedan, I remember our father
alone in the street with a billfold,
waving *come back* and crying.

Father's Mail-Order Rifles

My father swore expensive scopes were junk.
Through binoculars, I saw limbs clipped
a hundred yards from deer across the meadow.
My father cursed and shot and missed again.
Once, he flung his rifle and struck me,

then shoved me down, stammering apologies.
When he was a boy in Flanders, my father
fought the Great War from a truck,
wobble-wheeled deliveries to the front.
My uncle taught him to kneel,

to cock his finger easy and not breathe,
then scoffed and strutted off. I hated
my uncle's bold tattoos, his walls
cluttered with trophies. I pitied the rifle
wobbling in my father's fists, his squinting eye.

I cursed him and ran away to the pickup,
hoping he wouldn't whirl and shoot me
in the back. I slapped at cactus
and laughed at rattlers in my path, knowing
he'd never hit whatever he aimed at.

Rodeo Bulls

The danger more than horns
is hooves in the belly,
a black, two-thousand-pound bull
intent on stomping. Nothing beats
being lucky, hard to stay on
a twisting tornado
snapping your spine
like a whip, hard to keep
your fingers crossed for luck,
fist cramped
on the hump
of his shoulders. A mad bull
moves more ways than one,
no guessing
when he coils
and lunges, anything to fling
the rag-doll body
off his back,
the fire of metal spurs
raking his belly. Half whale,
half killer shark, he leaps
and fishtails in the dust
and blood of the rodeo,
wild eyed,
foaming at the mouth,
dying for someone
to crush.

The Clink of Brown Bottles

We toasted luck with the clink of brown bottles
shaped like clubs, swaggered past tables
and asked some city strangers to dance.
Billy Ray and I leaned on our elbows,

twisting around in deerskin chairs
like studying broncs in a rodeo, guessing
the balance of meat and muscle, the fight
between the eyes, the toss of blonde hair

meaning go, back when regret was a word
we suffered casually, swaggering away,
trying to hide our wounded pride with spurs
that jingled back to the table,

the devil take that stuck-up blonde
with her pounds of mascara and her paunchy lover—
so old he'd probably never been to a war
and hated everyone but her.

Riding Herd

Barbed wires on rusted nails can't hold
lone bulls at home when they smell pasture.
They thrust their bone skulls under barbs,
tongues quivering for a taste of strange

and shove until the post gives way. Days later,
we find wires sagging, reset the post,
and tighten bent wires like a fiddle
and rope the worn-out bull,

wishing there was only a fence
between us and our hearts' desire.
But something with spurs and a rope
would find us, cursing and yelling on horseback,

cutting us off from escape down arroyos,
dragging us frothing and wild-eyed
back to the sun-bleached yellow range,
the same whirlpool of buzzards.

The Rockets' Red Glare

Trapped in a sandbagged bunker,
I hummed old country and western tunes
to explosions louder than my ears
could stand, the rhythms of Nashville
all that saved me from rockets
driving us all insane. Caught in a war

we left home hoping to survive,
we huddled in underwear, concussions
and sirens calling us to the noise
of this world. Cold and bunkered down
and whining George Jones love songs,
we stared at sandbags, already buried,

cursing an all-clear horn that never came
until the songs I knew were sung
and still the siren wailed
and rockets burst like jokes
people I didn't know kept telling
in an airplane about to crash.

III. Roll Call

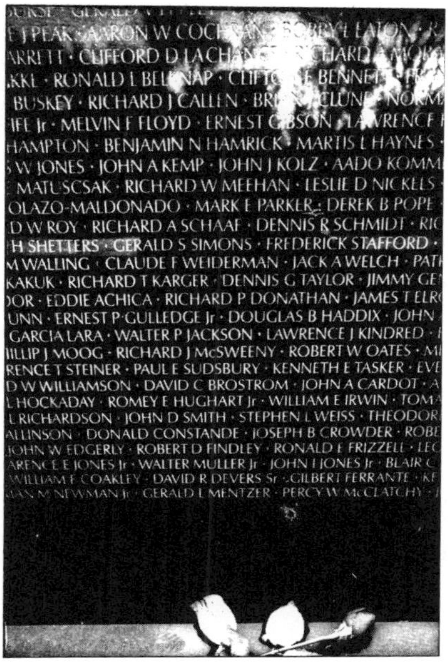

The Signs of Prairie Rattlers

The days of rattlesnakes are back,
fat rattlers on every trail. All day in the saddle
I see jackrabbits to wide horizons. Out here,
the eyes don't believe in signs. I shove sticks down
to make mad rattlers strike, snare them with wires

and cage them. Not one more rattle can save them
from the fire. I never believed the claims
of snake charmers in carnivals and church.
I've heard mad preachers claim this sand
is like the Bible deserts. They quoted Moses

with serpents impaled on poles. Watch signs,
they warned with spitting tongues—coyotes
trying to mate with your dogs at noon,
a mirage that shimmers at dawn, lost owls
without a barn in daylight. They prophesied

a thousand years of peace. Back from a war,
I've found rattlers mangled at dawn,
eyeless in Gaza. I've seen coyotes
lame in the hip and starving, risking the ranch
in daylight. I've cut a window in our wall

to save barn owls from cats. Our rafters are an ark
for owls. I have faith in most home remedies—
hard work and red-eye chili and homespun love.
Prophets in revival tents when I was five
are dead or mumbling in retirement homes.

I've heard them preaching to themselves in shawls
in rocking chairs they haven't the power to move.
I've seen their stares, starved for faith
in more than serpents, their folded hands,
their blinking, hollow eyes.

Counting Survivors

I'm stunned to see so many of us home.
I drive downtown to shout hosanna quietly,
pipe organ booming. The padded church bench
shudders like a medevac on takeoff.
Saigon falls often in my dreams.

I see sad others on TV on cycles
roaring toward the wall, or leaning down in greens
and jungle boots. Most friends I knew
are back in body. I miss good friends
who earned this service. I've faced the wall

and placed my fingers on their names.
I wish for Easter all year long.
I watch parades from curbs
and wonder how do survivors live?
How do the dead arise?

Uncle Philip and the Endless Names

Uncle Philip hated work, walked off a dozen jobs
before thirty. Wide jaw, sharp teeth, he sported
a wiry moustache and smoked, believed the sisters
from Bovina who called him handsome.
He remembered their names when he was eighty.

His mother died when he was ten,
years before he enlisted. Never mind the war,
the Kaiser's army of millions. Uncle Philip
won it over and over, his doubled fists like tanks.
Smoking, he coughed what he claimed

was mustard gas, the trenches of France
killing him. He lingered sixty years
with cigars, the pension he never got
stuck in his craw, his quarrel with the war
all that saved him from steady work.

I remember the tilt of his cap
in pictures, a Texas doughboy in Paris
caught with some girl he never saw again.
He taught me to toss a hook between logs
in the shallows, how to find bass in a dozen lakes.

He taught me to drive, slouched in his truck and smoking,
coaxed me to shift those gears like butter, don't lean
into turns but trust them, believing all eighteen wheels
would follow. When I glanced back in the mirror,
they followed. I remember his eyes in the rest home.

I followed his stare to the ceiling,
the shapeless water stains. Pointing,
he called forgotten names like a roll call,
soldiers I'd only heard of,
girls from Bovina, *Mother, Mother.*

The Hairpin Curve at Durango

Where the road dipped back on itself
downhill, I slowed the rig
so I wouldn't jackknife

or sail off into space.
That turn had killed runaway trucks,
smashed on the stones below,

convertibles and fast sports cars
careening smartly out
and tumbling. Truckers I knew

didn't dread crashing head-on
with drivers who fall asleep
on the straightaway,

didn't mind running sassy pickups
off the road, the devil
and bar ditch take them.

But icy roads that curve
and slide us helpless into air
are trouble. Dieseling downhill,

I bluffed oncoming traffic
to the rails, no way I'd risk the edge
for courtesy. Climbing home,

groaning with a load of calves,
I ground uphill, my right wheels
safe on asphalt,

making poor guys creeping downhill
hug the centerline.
Knowing the gray sky twisted

and disappeared inches away
below them, I glanced
at their wide eyes, their fists

knuckled on their wheels.
I saw their tight lips yelling
at their kids, *Shut up. Shut up.*

Uncle Jerry and the Velvet Dog

Uncle Jerry lost a fortune and won it back
a thousand times, hunched on his elbows,
knuckles and blunt nails taunting, tapping the bait.
Men rob each other blind with their eyes,
bluffing their way to money. Storm doors he promised
had to wait till Labor Day after the rains.
Aunt Martha's wrath hung like a sword above him.

By Halloween, he brought home bathroom tiles
and had the roof ripped off, installed plush carpet
for her corns, a velvet dog in the corner
with silver dollar eyes, big as a bear,
something stuffed she could pet which didn't bark
when Jerry's key hit the latch after midnight.
Christmas came without a tree or tinsel gifts.

Martha draped the dog with baubles, star on his nose
like Rudolph. Jerry found her one night in the alley
dragging the dog through the snow and weeping,
trying to cram that velvet dog in a dumpster
with other trash, fluorescent in moonlight,
its buckshot eyes bouncing each time
she shoved and punched it in the face.

The Tap of Angry Reins

The last day of the month, and I can't make
friends meet. Sullen, they'd rather quarrel.
Bury the proof and let debates go begging.
We buy back nothing we give away with the tongue,

the quickest organ, that tap of angry reins
on a mule. Miles from the nearest road,
we sit in a jeep surrounded by derricks of oil,
the bones of quarrels like dinosaurs.

Even with carbon dating we can't name them,
feuds the way to graveyards of old friends.
Sometimes it's thunder, voices so loud
the dog shakes, wetting himself, his eyes begging.

After a lashing, the tongue is bleached
like cow bones. Even deep wells dry up,
plains where discouraging words come easier
than drought. Ears believe whatever they are told.

Quarrels are mesquite trees ranchers bulldoze
and burn for pastures. In spite of tractors
and chain saws, still the deep roots grow back,
spreading, tangled with the roots of others.

If little words led goats to market,
we'd all be rich. They turn up centuries later
when our own best schemes are ribs and skulls.
Bulls gorge all night in the mind's silo.

Bloated at dawn, they blow their red-eyed breath
across the room and lower pointed horns,
snorting, pawing the dust. Bury the dead
and let good fences save us, if they can.

Farms at Auction

Bidders from out of state drop by and stare.
They kick our neighbor's clods
and wade mirages like walking on water.
My barn a mile away appears to burn.

My neighbor's barbed wires shimmer,
his cattle blur, about to disappear.
Three years hailed out, he's quitting,
enough debt to break his children,

enough silage in his silo to feed one winter cow.
The auctioneer calls *gimme, gimme,*
all he owns gone twice and sold,
even the dirt, the oaks his father planted.

I remember summer clouds a mile away,
bubbles a dozen churches prayed for.
I envied his rain, the downpour I wanted,
nothing but thunder for my parched stalks.

I didn't hear the hail, too busy cursing rain
to count my blessings. Sheered off,
his stubble rots. His beds are gone,
his trunks and keepsakes, hauled off to town

in a trailer returned to the farm for auction.
The man with wide suspenders kisses a bullhorn,
a sideshow barker. And loaded with luck
we gather close and watch some bidder

poke our neighbor's plows and tractor,
his wife's best tablecloths
like touching her robes and dresses
to satisfy himself they're silk.

Scanning the Range for Strays

Granddaddy roamed these fields
in a pickup, scanning the range for strays
lost in arroyos. If a steer was alive,
he'd find it. Roped, it balked

but followed that smoking truck uphill,
walleyed and frothing. They don't make trucks
that coarse anymore, no radio,
a bench of steel coils covered by quilts.

There it rusts, stranded on blocks
where we hauled it. I remember
Granddaddy's white mustache,
the scar where a roped bull hooked him.

I remember the boulder he straddled
driving out of the canyon. Stalled,
he must have bounced on the bumper
until his heart stopped. We found him

face down in the dust, the steer
snugged to the truck and foaming,
no longer jerking, the rope
so tight we had to cut it loose.

Hardscrabble, Tooth and Claw

Packs roam the plains, attacking abandoned pets.
Caught in the fields, most cats survive.
They scratch the eyes of dogs, the pack
maddened by blood. I've come across cats
before the buzzards found them, and blind dogs

stumbling and whining. I pack a rifle
even for starving bobcats. Owls don't ask
who did it. My wife's green eyes glean kittens
from our fields like picking lint off cashmere.
Today, we found another sackful by the road,

a litter tossed from a car, scraps for the buzzards.
When we're in time, my wife nurses cats
with eyedroppers, milk from a holstein.
They grow up gladly in our barn, stalking mice
on claws grown perfect, their purring mouths all fangs.

Witching on Canvas

With horsehairs dipped in oils
she scatters our lean cattle
deep into pebbles of canvas,
witches mesquite and cactus
from hardpan caliche white.

I've watched oil borders dry
while she draws babies' baths
and irons real clothes in summer.
In times of fever
she goes without sleep,

without a brush in her hand for weeks,
and then like cracks in the crust
of last year's drought,
she draws windmills and streams
and makes them flow.

Rembrandt and the Art of Mercy

They say the luster of gold addicted him
to fat, round guilders' purses.
They claim his florid nose exposed
a painter's lust, that even the scent of stiff,
splayed bristles glazed with oils aroused him,

and skin like honey on the tongue
provoked him, made him pose models sweating
till they wept. They claim he painted haunted faces,
that nothing glistens but their hats and helmets.
No, what he loved and pitied most was flesh

that's caught but never saved by canvas. Consider
his florid elders astounded by Susanna bathing,
his naked Danaë with her god of gold. Behold
the fragile, eggshell flesh of sad Bathsheba,
her toes and thighs scrubbed slowly

for a king. If only he could capture those
in ocher, rub her troubled eyes so they could see.
Notice the gold, pig-bristle swirls that touched
his dying Saskia's neck, her honey lobes,
the sweaty radiance of her breasts.

The Dust We're Made Of

All summer under klieg lights
we stroked the dirt with trowels.
Those digs would disappear, vandals
and idle boys playing plunder: an arrowhead
wedged in a faded Levi pocket, a jawbone mocked

and tossed away like a corncob,
a hand-smoothed bowl crushed to dust by a boot.
We unfolded sand like castle tapestries,
layer by layer down to mammoths
and bears the size of bulls.

We found bronze kernels never baked,
like golden ears hung up to dry
on southwest porches. We had eaten tortillas
of such crushed corn. Here, people like us
lay down in darkness. We sifted dust

we were made of. What did they fear?
Near midnight on our knees
we cataloged clues for regional museums,
the signs of modest toil, evidence of hope
not seen, the kernels not consumed.

Names on the Wrists of Strangers

Pity mere flesh and tongues, but never
tungsten alloys in the wings of jets.
Tons missing in action are cans
flipped from cars on highways,

not bodies of pilots. Did he ride
a spinning F-4 Phantom down,
welded to wreckage? Or eject and walk away?
Does he know petitions are still being begged

for his release, even one word of condolence,
Dead? Could he dream of bracelets
with his name on the wrists of strangers,
reaching for phones that never ring:

the dial tone's there,
but no one calls. We long to believe
he haunts us with flesh we will touch,
not forever hostage to whatever whim

keeps men imprisoned twenty years
and beats them. Let him learn the ways
of snakes and survive, a legend
Montagnards will whisper for years.

Some evening on the news, when the lens
zooms down to a deck of refugees from Laos
or Da Nang, the boat wallowing on waves
near Hong Kong, let one of the faces be his.

IV. Under Blue Skies

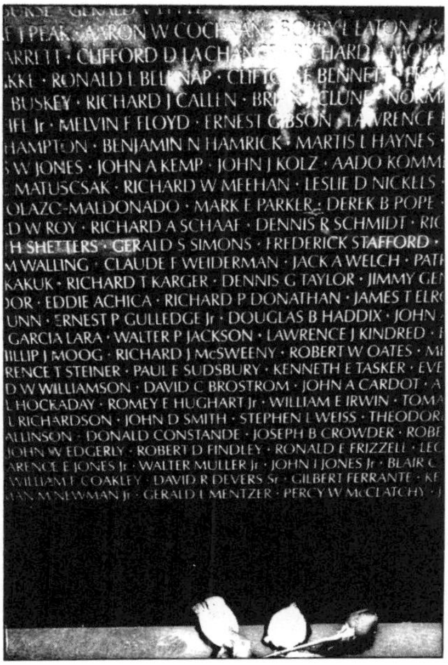

Neighbors Miles Away

Blistering heat shimmers our fields
like lakes. It seldom rains.
Surveyors rode here in 1880 hungover,
swearing they'd mapped these miles before,
cursing sextants and starving comancheros

who left these plains to settlers.
Coronado's army crossed four hundred years ago,
coughing, praying for clouds, crossing themselves
and grumbling, tugging their stumbling
Spanish mares, rumors of gold

on their minds, a thousand miles
from leaky galleons anchored in the Gulf.
Our wells flood the dung and hoof prints
of their route. We pump the purest water
three hundred feet to grain

they never dreamed could grow.
This sky is what they saw,
these level fields. We're not alone.
When we drive flat roads to town,
neighbors miles away look up and wave.

At the Rattlesnake Roundup

A thousand rattlers strike the names of captors
dropped into slots by boys in cowboy boots.
In fields where it hasn't rained since Eden,
we scoured the range for signs,

sweating in fields the rattlers own,
reaping venom for doctors—toddlers attacked
at the park, old people bending down
for radishes, shocked by a slash of fangs.

Mining for fangs like diamonds,
we jerked dry tumbleweeds aside.
Coiled lightning was on our mind,
the fastest draw surviving. Caught,

a rattler thrashes like a wildcat
trying to twist away, hating people
who won't toss it back to the briar patch
until they bruise its head, fangs locked

on a mason jar, venom like lies
squeezed out, the old serpent
dropped in a cage to rattle
at every human in sight.

Father's Wild Pheasants

My father came back bored, too many pheasants
in the fields, the sheen of green and bronze
in every row of stubble. When he was a boy,
the nearest pheasants nested four counties west.

He shot the first on our ranch when I was ten
and made me clean it. Feathers clung to my skin
like static, intestines ruptured by buckshot.
I carried the stench for days. For Christmas

he gave me a twenty gauge, taught me
to draw an oiled cloth slowly through the barrel.
When pheasants nested in our fields,
he called lost cousins to bring their guns.

For years they came, stalking wild cocks
in ranks, rows of cousins reaping our fields,
the boom and flash like muskets
along a half-mile front. Then Uncle Ernest

died of cancer, Claude in a car wreck.
One season, only my brother and I
took to the fields, bagging our limit easy
in cold wind gusting from the north

in sight of the swing where he rested,
rocking, whittling some duck decoy,
the nearest lake a hundred miles away.
Noon, we found him hunched on the porch

without a hat, twisting the wood
augur-eyed, rubbing his thumb on the grain
as if looking for clues to the future,
his stiff hair whipping in the wind.

Nights on the Porch Swing

I see from my wife's green eyes
we're not alone. Our stock tank
shimmers in moonlight. Whatever warns her

makes her squeeze my neck—a whiff of fear,
a riffle of feathers. Owls own the earth,
round eyes thrust downward. I've seen her

rescue five baby ducks a day, a night-light on
for ducks waddling spoiled in the washroom.
On the swing, I talk of hunger,

the natural curve of talons. *Hush,*
she warns me. Her body knows the rhythms
of the moon, expects owls most nights

and ignores them. Tonight, her fingers
strum the short hairs of my neck.
We hear a scream squeezed out by talons.

I shove the porch swing higher with my boots,
but her moccasins stop us,
dragging the swing off balance. *Hush,*

she says, her nails in my flesh.
She tugs my beard and squeezes,
her fingers stroking, stroking my neck.

Dogs in the World They Own

This is the call for order on a farm,
dogs barking at cars and pickups on the road.
Any post inside the fence, they own,
wetting the weeds, the shadows of clouds.

Skunks waddle up and die in their own scent
sprayed at the fangs of mad dogs
ripping them apart. Coyotes know
which fields have dogs, and lope for miles.

Sometimes a prowling cat hears snarling
too close to outrun and climbs the only pole
in sight. Dogs trot and bark for hours.
The hot sun melts their tongues.

Even when dogs lie down, the cat stays there
all night, stares at my wife
who comes at dawn coaxing with water,
a saucer of milk. The cat blinks,

cramped like a skull on the post. And then
one dawn it's gone, the dogs patrolling
their dirt, hawks hunting overhead,
all gates and grazing cows in place.

The Meaning of Flat Fields

Landscape never tells us how to live
in the world. It never moves,
is moved, shifted in sandstorms,
silted by floods, thrust up as mountains

and cliffs millions of years ago.
Nothing that cold teaches us how to cope
with blood. We tell a landscape
what we hope it means, invent rich sounds

wise as well as ancient and give those
mournful names to landscapes—ocean,
horizon, stone. Nothing
that long ago knew what to do

but kill and flee from being eaten.
We've hurled the fear in ourselves
to the moon, our longing for peace
into sunsets. Hawks are no wiser

for watching the world from above,
no safer than rabbits balled up
in burrows, crouched with wide eyes,
not knowing when to run.

Coyotes and Dogs

Uncle Earl kept a Saint Bernard in his tavern
before the state law banned it, the patron dog
of his dance hall. My knuckles knew his rubber lips,
his purple tongue, thick double chins stuffed with fur.
He clung like a python when I scratched him,

digging my fist in his ribs. Cowboys taught him
to howl sad tunes with the jukebox. Girls tossed him
quarters, the only dog on the dance floor,
waddling past couples locked in each other's arms.
Lapping draft beer, he lay down by blondes

and cowboys who tugged off leather gloves
and let him lick stiff knuckles busted in rodeos.
Fists that shot wild dogs and coyotes
burrowed into folds of fur and made
his massive paw keep time, thumping the floor.

I remember how he howled and tugged outside
after the sheriff left, the moon no jukebox,
a dozen pickups but not one fist to pet him,
sniffing packs of coyotes miles away,
dragging the stiff chain tight.

Nights Without Rockets

Goats keep us fed, bless them for butting.
They jab sharp horns between barbed wires
and climb our plows like ladders.
They leap the fence into acres of oats

like locusts, dancing on sheds like circus dogs,
hopping on shaggy legs to nibble pears,
afraid of nothing. The bark is gone, all leaves
they can reach. Grandfather worked these plains

for steers, alert for rustlers. Last night
I heard an old board crack, too loud for prowlers.
My flashlight nailed a billy stalking the barn.
I watched him bluff the stuttering owls,

butting the door. I swore I'd sow these fields
and let crops grow, but I lie here
counting nights without rockets,
knowing goats wander the yard,

thankful for only odor, no shots,
no madness anywhere they strut. Goats cough,
hoping for trouble. They stomp,
an audition of beards vain and impatient.

They've never gone to war,
drag no load of guilt into nightmare.
I've watched them roam for hours in moonlight,
jabbing their horns like sabers at the dark.

To All Friends Fast Asleep

Rest, heads twisted severely
on your necks, or muffled facedown
or on your sides, jaws
drawn to the chests, legs up,
bones of shoulders and hips

burrowed into pine needles of sleep,
or staked out flat on your backs,
chins slack, exhausted
by the weight of space
shoved down, shoved down all day

on hands that lift
and pat each other on the back,
or simply grip and squeeze,
handshakes that mean *Hello,*
hold on, it's over, it's okay.

On Taking a Grandson Hunting

Only later, as he approached
expecting nothing breathing
in feathers he aimed at,

but something flat like pelts
on highways—fearing no evil.
At least with its eyes closed.

And most lay still.
Woodcarvings.
Nothing like doves.

In his sleeping bag in the camper
all night he tried to forget
the one dove bleeding

with eyes like a kitten,
the throat rapidly beating,
the dark pearls.

The Invention of Courage

The slam and cable whine of dawn.
Nothing in dreams prepares us
for such noise, the rumble and bang
down side streets. In alleys,
at loading docks and trash cans, trucks tug
and bump the morning out to sea. We rise
and drive to work, checking the clock,
amazed another day has gone, whistling
as if we've passed the date line.

At drive-in movies in Dumas
in high school, on hay scattered on beds
of pickups, we strained to watch monsters
with scales invading cities, devouring bullets
and maidens. Nothing stopped raw hunger
we understood. Buried in straw,
we felt the climax of robots
explode on the screen, a good time
to comb straw from our hair
like rubble, blinded by lights
at intermission, hungry and hot,
wild to go out among our kind.

When we were kids
inventing courage, we crouched,
gouging fire with sticks whittled
like spears. We listened to brothers
hiss of witches and wolves
in the darkness, billions of stars
lighting nothing but ghosts.
To stop their terrible lies
we chased each other around
and around the bonfire,
swinging our blazing sticks.

Charts

We didn't believe the stars
slashing across our years meant anything
but Orion hunting seven stars he never found,
a parade of unattainable maidens,
the tilted dipper pouring nothing.

We claimed we understood the hunger
of a bear lumbering under the North Star,
longed for the dawning of the age of Aquarius.
With luck we survived a war, the raising
of children and monthly debts, so far.

And now we've come this side of fifty,
a puzzled hunter stiff in the joints
and faithful wife stumbling somewhere under a maze
of stars, Polaris only a name for navigation
whose mutable charts we can't use

wherever we're going, dippers tipping
toward the grave. Father of light,
we can't dread outer darkness where burning stars
hurtle outward, a gallery of myths,
but beg more light in this created world.

Geldings on Mountain Ranches

Horses in barns survive the cold on oats
trucked up from town, vacation from tourists
who pay to kick their ribs in spring
and jerk them nervously on trails.

Switchbacks a thousand feet straight down
are nothing to geldings lifting bristled tails.
They pass stale gas to each other like code,
clopping iron shoes single file up mountains

one hoof at a time. Climbing is all they do
under tight-lipped people they'll never save again.
They take two extra steps before turning, the gasps
and squeezing knees well worth the jolt of bits

twisting them back from the edge, uphill.
They know how close to the ledge they can go,
how many times before the wrangler scolds them.
If they remember loping green pastures,

the bucking days before castration, hay muzzles them
after a day of trails, stroking their tongues over oats.
They never nod for strangers patting their rumps,
Nice horse. Tourists smooth their necks and whisper

Sweetheart, digging in tight Levi's for sugar cubes
crushed to powder, grateful to be alive after cliffs
where they might have died but for these steeds,
these massive, muscled legs.

Letting Go

Raised on the plains, we believed
in bald horizons where the sun burned
every crop. We clung to the myth

the world is flat under skies so dry
weeds wilt. Buzzards glided
always in sight, and rattlers coiled

in our yard. Born in the Rockies,
our babies climbed before they could walk,
their eyes brimming with trees.

The steepest roofs were dwarfed,
and snakes draped above us on boulders.
The spoor of cougars tempted our children

to climb, to wander off. They scaled
mountain peaks, breathing thin air
they evolved to, believing wilderness

was the world, and that bears
owned no more of the woods
than our children prowled

miles from the hearth where we stayed
stoking embers, sweeping,
oiling the locks.

Grace and the Blood of Goats

Ghosts of old prospectors pick up their beds
and walk, but even here we're safe.
I hear you swear your faith in mountains,
snow reflecting nothing we have at home.

We need what prairie eyes don't hope for,
that isn't ours to feed. The owls wear feathered chaps
like prairie hawks we know, night riders over sage
and cactus. Come back to bed and ignore them.

The moon is silver beaten thin. Together
we'll tease away trick knees that lock,
bifocal eyes that open early. We salvage nothing
we gave away, wasted in hours of overtime,

trying to make the dust we are
yield more than rushed fumbling after a shower, then back
to cactus and goats spraying a trail of pellets.
A man I flew with went to the moon and home,

a hero riding a rocket aimed at no one.
That was years ago, after I flew back from Saigon.
Crossing a log today, we stared at water tumbling fast.
Don't look, I said, as if blind faith could save us.

We confess everything takes luck, even a friend's
jaunty steps on a moon we're staring at. Tonight,
even if we call to it, peace, be still, the moon
keeps bleaching before our eyes. We wait for grace

in a world deserted, where the blood of goats
can't save us. The babies we raised were worth it,
but now we're alone, lost in a snow field at night
in mountains. Tonight, we swear we'll worship flesh

and tongues with more patient ears, but never again
mere goats grazing flat plains where nothing changes
but names chiseled on marble. We know
we won't change much, but anyway we swear.

Under Blue Skies

I see what the horse sees,
a whirling funnel of wings
in slow motion. I know

what I'll find, if I ride there,
the horse not willing to back talk.
Whatever it was, it's over,

no more desire or fear forever—
a calf that wandered off
down crumbling shale,

unable to bawl loud enough
until it starved. Or only a rabbit
that outlived the rattlers,

the safest death, simply to lie down
under blue skies and sleep, accepting
this as the way, not dreading anything.

V. Time for the Traction of Docks

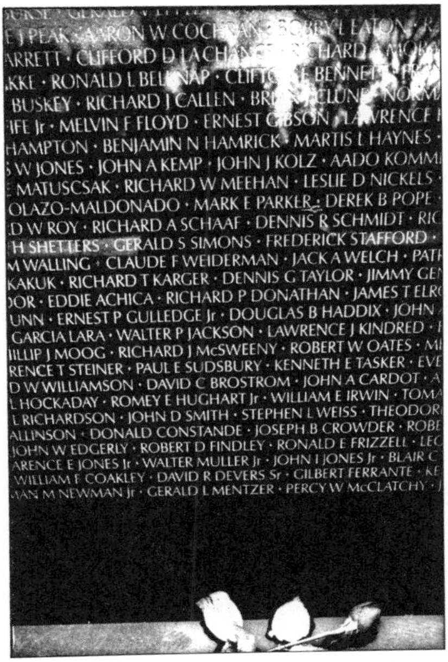

Time for the Traction of Docks

I've stopped wading for trout in Montana.
Time for the traction of docks thrust boldly
onto lakes, like bridges going nowhere.
Now let them come to dinner, granddaddy catfish
cruising the bottom, crappie forever hungry.

This rig my grandkids gave is all crossbeams
and swivels, a mobile of silver hooks. I'll take
whatever bites. Who needs the battle of bass
in the shallows? Fish eager to believe in bait
confess their faith in trinkets. I reel them in,

doffing my cap to grandkids screaming and laughing.
They hug me as if I'm feeding thousands,
blessing their gift with magic. I let them feel
the quivering crappie, the mica scales.
If it's a catfish, I grit my teeth and reel,

bowing my back to raise a rod bent double. They gasp,
their wide eyes shine. Keeping the sharp barbs
covered, I let them touch the slippery tail,
the rubber lips. If the fish swallowed it all,
even needle-nose pliers can't tease out a hook

without ripping. Holding the squirming fish
out of sight, I point at hovering gulls or a speedboat
splashing by, while I tug or cut the line,
time in another summer to show how much
a catfish suffers, how rough old men must be.

Rocking for Days in the Shade

In another parched summer,
comancheros gone, we rock
on the back porch, fanning,
watching buzzards circle like clocks,

calling their lazy cousins to supper.
We sip iced tea, rolling cold glasses
on our skin. Not one thick cloud
for months, the weeds so brittle

goats snap them off like sticks.
We wonder, are we here by choice?
Great-grandfather left the cavalry
for this? After renegade bullets and arrows

he stayed in Texas where topsoil was sand
and free. He said he needed sun to heal.
The only blood he lost in forty years
dried on rocks already red.

These goats are not his goats.
Imported rams he bred were sterile,
cotton the way he kept from starving.
When he stumbled on this canyon

in smelly blues on horseback,
chasing the last straggling
comanchero raiders
off the plains of Texas,

he retired—a hidden range,
enough water to bathe in,
far enough from others
to build a shack with a back porch

and do whatever he wanted, rocking for days
in the shade, watching buzzards thirsty
for his blood, daring anything
to make him leave.

Living in Old Adobe

A moon like this is money. Fat cattle
believe it's dawn, grazing by the barn,
addicted to alfalfa. The moon is ripe
for coyotes. Skunks waddle boldly by,
pretending we can't see them, two by two

into darkness. The porch swing groans
on hooks as old as us. Granddaddy
built this porch to last, oak planks
imported from forests. How many nights
did they rock here, seeing the stars we see?

Did they hope a burly grandson
would hold his own wife close on chains
we didn't hang? Now we're their age,
or older. Grandchildren we adore
are sleeping tonight in Dallas.

They dream in beds and cradle, starlight
flooding their ark. Dolls and bears
are locked in their arms, animals we gave,
accepting these creaking chains,
coyotes a mile away, all waddling skunks.

Stalls in All Weather

Deep inside silos,
layers of spoilage ripen
vinegar-sweet, stubble of sticky maize
fermenting wine for cows. They love
the bitter stalks, the half-digested
casserole of sap and fiber.

They loll those foot-long toothpicks
in their lips, grind them with grain
and swallow. Cows stare at snow fields
white as cream. If they remember calves,
the shudder of bulls at breeding,
they find relief in hunger.

They lower heads like gourds
and scoop dark silage like manna,
full udders bulging,
grasped in the predawn cold,
the clang of gates and tug of suction
all they need for now.

Luck of the Draw

Witching on dry land is prophecy,
and drilling a well, creation.
Pipes of our neighbors' wells dry up,
and they auction all they own.
We seed each angry cloud
and dance each dance with weather.

When it's time to irrigate dry crops,
we crank an old Ford engine
and pump the purest water
up from nothing we've ever seen,
pouring our luck over fields
flat as the moon.

The Ogallala aquifer drops
three feet each season,
and nothing we know brings water
out of stone. Home is a casino
of chance and choice,
four arms that hold each other.

Someday

Horse thief or lover,
or merely innocent squatter?
What posse knotted the noose
and tossed it over?

Why shouldn't it be this tree,
grooves in the bark like rope burns?
Imagine a cocked neck bowed,
the hanged man's boots on tiptoe,

fists tied behind him.
Imagine a thousand thieves
swinging the same ballet.
Hear the twist of ropes under tension.

Why shouldn't it be this posse
galloping out of a canyon,
black hats and puffs of pistol shots?
Even from here I know their mounts

are mustangs, able to chase me
till sundown. They're in no hurry
but coming, five, no, six of them
twirling new ropes and shouting.

Saying the Blessing

I can't say anything new to children
on their own. They need my blessing
as I wanted my own father's love,
but nothing more—no roof

or weekly allowance, no easy advice.
I'd say it all again, abridged
and edited, if they'd let me,
convinced the old songs are the best—

the thunder of prairie rain,
the sober mourning of doves,
the joy of work in the wings
of hummingbirds, the holy Psalms.

When the Children Have Gone

What could we say, for they heard rumors:
something was out there that shouldn't be,
futures only they must own.
They rose on silver wings and disappeared,
far from summer sun on prairies.

Driving back after a week with grandkids,
we pass the asphalt hours by naming pelts
of flattened rattlers, coyotes,
crushed armadillos. What needs a meal
clacks its beak and staggers oddly off

into the sun, fat belly sagging,
black wings flapping a tight
possessive spiral back to bones
belly up under the thump of tires
with nothing better to do than swerve.

Back home, we listen to coyotes howling
the song we've sung for years. We live on beans
and *fajitas* braised over mesquite roots,
red peppers that scald our tongues. At dusk,
we carry chairs outside and watch the sundown.

My wife believes in the peace of dark,
the burning stars. I watch light shimmer
on her face, her flashing eyes. Now it begins,
the golds and purple on the plains. Blink
and miss it, like flecks of silver in her hair.

Leaving Sixty

Riding flat, hardscrabble plains,
we hold the reins of geldings
with fingers stiff in leather gloves.
The sun burns mirages blue as oceans:
shanghaied, we're trapped in a fleet
of boats, these creaky bones.

Charming Columbus, his scrolls
rolled into a globe, his tales of gold
and spice enticing. Look ahoy,
they're dropping off the horizon,
old friends once young as Columbus.
The world is flat: Isabella's fool

proved that by dying, leaving a skull,
the only gold of a dunce.
Columbus found the edge of the earth
years later, and no charts
or spinning globe could save him.
Only his nurse saw the old man vanish.

Far from port, my wife and I
wave semaphores of love
like *Santa Maria* scrolls:
We're headed west, loaded with gold
and spice, stiff riggings locked,
no way to shift the sails.

Mesas I Never Took the Time to Climb

I nudge this sweating gelding with my knees.
Old leather creaks as I lean between mesquite
and cactus. Our crops are rattlers and starry skies
we pretend are diamonds. My wife must know I'm coming,
lights bright in the kitchen. We live in a bowl of sand,

ten miles to any mesa. Coyotes prowl at night,
thinking we're fools to roam boldly in daylight.
Dawn, I shove old boots through stirrups and ride away,
content in a saddle, that perfect slap of leather chaps.
Torn gloves I've worn to brand castrated calves

still fit, no way I'd throw away a glove
because it's ugly. Hawks see no farther
than I could see from a mesa. The view is there,
if I want it. Today I found a buzzard in the field,
too weak to flap away. Panting, it hobbled

as if on stilts, others above us
wheeling a slow blessing on flesh. Will it miss
the soaring, the glide toward wide horizons?
Someday soon, I'll cut the fences down and let the bulls
run wild. I'll ride my gelding straight toward a mesa

I never took the time to climb. I'll dismount
and slap the sorrel to send him back to the corral.
I'll look at these flat fields from far above,
the same parched sand and cactus after sundown,
night shining not with diamonds, but real stars.

Acknowledgments

The author and publisher wish to acknowledge the following publications in which earlier versions of these poems first appeared, some with different titles: *The American Scholar* ("The Hairpin Curve at Durango," "Seconds of Free-Fall and Chaos"); *Artful Dodge* ("Names on the Wrists of Strangers," formerly "For Friends Missing in Action"); *The Atlantic* ("Heirlooms"); *Berkeley Poetry Review* ("Rodeo Bulls"); *Blue Unicorn* ("On Taking a Grandson Hunting," formerly "On Taking a Small Son Hunting"); *Carolina Quarterly* ("Nights on the Porch Swing," formerly "Leaving the Middle Years"); *Clockwatch Review* ("Saying the Blessing"); *College English* ("Fame at Eleven," "Grace and the Blood of Goats," "Leaving Sixty," formerly "Leaving the Middle Years," "Riding Herd," formerly "Riding on Hardscrabble"); *The Connecticut Poetry Review* ("Neighbors Miles Away," formerly "Living on Open Plains"); *Crosscurrents* ("Witching on Canvas"); *The Dalhousie Review* ("What If I Didn't Die Outside Saigon"); *Descant (Canada)* ("Stalls in All Weather," formerly "Stalls and the Laws of Order"); *The Florida Review* ("Boys with Chihuahua Dogs"); *The G.W. Review* ("At the Rattlesnake Roundup"); *The Georgia Review* ("Nights Without Rockets"); *Grand Street* ("Dogs in the World They Own"); *Hampden-Sydney Poetry Review* ("Father's Wild Pheasants"); *Hollins Critic* ("After the Fall of Saigon"); *Mānoa* ("Buzzards and Uncle Douglas," "Harvest," formerly "Farms and the Laws of Harvest," "The Price They Paid for Range," formerly "Living on Open Range"); *Maryland Poetry Review* ("Counting Survivors"); *Michigan Quarterly Review* ("The Tap of Angry Reins," formerly "Quarrels and the Laws of Mercy"); *Mississippi Review* ("The Clink of Brown Bottles," formerly "When It Seemed Easy"); *Mississippi Valley Review* ("For Friends Missing in Action"); *The Missouri Review* ("Farms at Auction," "The Invention of Courage," "Scanning the Range for Strays," "The Signs of Prairie Rattlers," "Uncle Philip and the Endless Names"); *The Nation* ("When the Children Have Gone," formerly "The Middle Years"); *The New Criterion* ("Someday," formerly "Leaving the Middle Years," "Under Blue Skies," formerly "Black Wings Wheeling"); *New England Review* ("Rembrandt and the Art of Mercy"); *New Texas 92* ("Out of the Stone They Come," formerly "On the Eve of War in the Persian Gulf," "Time for the Traction of Docks," formerly "Old Men Fishing at Brownwood"); *The New York Review of Books* ("Digging in a Footlocker"); *Ontario Review* ("My Brother and the Golden Gloves," formerly "After A Year in Korea"); *The Paris Review* ("Rocking for Days in the Shade," formerly "Goat Ranching on Hardscrabble"); *Pequod* ("The Meaning of Flat Fields"); *Poem* ("Living in Old Adobe," formerly "The Middle Years"); *Poet & Critic* ("Coyotes and Dogs," "Regular Programming on the Eve of War"); *Poetry* ("The Dust We're Made Of," formerly "The Digs in Escondido Canyon," and "Wishing for More than Thunder"); *Poetry Durham* ("The Rockets' Red Glare"); *Prairie Schooner* ("Letting Go"); *Santa Clara Review* ("War in the Persian Gulf"); *The Seattle Review* ("To All Friends Fast Asleep"); *Shenandoah* ("The Gleam of Silver Wings"); *South Coast Poetry Journal* ("Life with Father"); *Southern Poetry Review* ("Mesas I Never Took the Time to Climb," formerly "Leaving the Middle Years"); and *Tar River Poetry* ("Charts," formerly "Stars and the Laws of Motion").

"Geldings on Mountain Ranges" is reprinted from *Kansas Quarterly,* 24: 2 & 3 1994. By permission of the publishers.

"Father's Mail-Order Rifles" is reprinted from *National Forum: The Phi Kappa Phi Journal,* Volume LXXIV, Number 1 (Winter 1994). Copyright © by Walter McDonald. By permission of the publishers.

"Luck of the Draw," formerly "Making Book on the Aquifer" was published in the *Sewanee Review,* Volume 97, Number 1, January-March 1989. Copyright © 1989 by Walter McDonald.

"Hardscrabble, Tooth and Claw" and "Teaching Our Sons Old Chores" were originally published in the *Windsor Review,* Vol. 27, No. 2 (Fall 1994), pp. 20-21.

I'm especially grateful to the National Endowment for the Arts and to Texas Tech University for time to write many of these poems.

Walter McDonald

is Paul Whitfield Horn Professor of English, poet in residence, and director of creative writing at Texas Tech University. He was a pilot in the U.S. Air Force, taught at the Air Force Academy, and served in Vietnam. He has a Ph.D. from the University of Iowa and has published fifteen collections of poetry and has had more than 1,200 poems published in journals. He has received National Endowment for the Arts Creative Writing Fellowships, the Juniper Prize, and the George Elliston Prize. Three of his books won the National Cowboy Hall of Fame's Western Heritage Award and three received the Texas Institute of Letters' Poetry Prize. He also received the President's Excellence in Teaching Award at Texas Tech and was selected by the Council for Advancement and Support of Education (CASE) as 1992 Texas Professor of the Year.

PITT POETRY SERIES

Ed Ochester, General Editor

Claribel Alegría, *Flowers from the Volcano*
Claribel Alegría, *Woman of the River*
Debra Allbery, *Walking Distance*
Maggie Anderson, *Cold Comfort*
Maggie Anderson, *A Space Filled with Moving*
Robin Becker, *Giacometti's Dog*
Siv Cedering, *Letters from the Floating World*
Lorna Dee Cervantes, *Emplumada*
Robert Coles, *A Festering Sweetness: Poems of American People*
Nancy Vieira Couto, *The Face in the Water*
Jim Daniels, *M-80*
Kate Daniels, *The Niobe Poems*
Kate Daniels, *The White Wave*
Toi Derricotte, *Captivity*
Sharon Doubiago, *South America Mi Hija*
Stuart Dybek, *Brass Knuckles*
Odysseus Elytis, *The Axion Esti*
Jane Flanders, *Timepiece*
Forrest Gander, *Lynchburg*
Richard Garcia, *The Flying Garcias*
Suzanne Gardinier, *The New World*
Gary Gildner, *Blue Like the Heavens: New & Selected Poems*
Elton Glaser, *Color Photographs of the Ruins*
Hunt Hawkins, *The Domestic Life*
Lawrence Joseph, *Curriculum Vitae*
Lawrence Joseph, *Shouting at No One*
Julia Kasdorf, *Sleeping Preacher*
Etheridge Knight, *The Essential Etheridge Knight*
Bill Knott, *Poems, 1963–1988*
Ted Kooser, *One World at a Time*
Ted Kooser, *Sure Signs: New and Selected Poems*
Ted Kooser, *Weather Central*
Larry Levis, *The Widening Spell of the Leaves*
Larry Levis, *Winter Stars*
Larry Levis, *Wrecking Crew*
Walter McDonald, *Counting Survivors*
Irene McKinney, *Six O'Clock Mine Report*
Archibald MacLeish, *The Great American Fourth of July Parade*
Peter Meinke, *Liquid Paper: New and Selected Poems*

Peter Meinke, *Night Watch on the Chesapeake*
Carol Muske, *Applause*
Carol Muske, *Wyndmere*
Leonard Nathan, *Carrying On: New & Selected Poems*
Kathleen Norris, *Little Girls in Church*
Ed Ochester and Peter Oresick, *The Pittsburgh Book of Contemporary American Poetry*
Sharon Olds, *Satan Says*
Gregory Orr, *City of Salt*
Alicia Suskin Ostriker, *Green Age*
Alicia Suskin Ostriker, *The Imaginary Lover*
Greg Pape, *Black Branches*
Greg Pape, *Storm Pattern*
Kathleen Peirce, *Mercy*
David Rivard, *Torque*
Liz Rosenberg, *Children of Paradise*
Liz Rosenberg, *The Fire Music*
Natasha Sajé, *Red Under the Skin*
Maxine Scates, *Toluca Street*
Richard Shelton, *Selected Poems, 1969–1981*
Reginald Shepherd, *Some Are Drowning*
Betsy Sholl, *The Red Line*
Peggy Shumaker, *The Circle of Totems*
Peggy Shumaker, *Wings Moist from the Other World*
Jeffrey Skinner, *The Company of Heaven*
Cathy Song, *School Figures*
Leslie Ullman, *Dreams by No One's Daughter*
Constance Urdang, *Alternative Lives*
Constance Urdang, *Only the World*
Michael Van Walleghen, *Tall Birds Stalking*
Ronald Wallace, *People and Dog in the Sun*
Ronald Wallace, *Time's Fancy*
Belle Waring, *Refuge*
Michael S. Weaver, *My Father's Geography*
Michael S. Weaver, *Timber and Prayer*
Robley Wilson, *Kingdoms of the Ordinary*
Robley Wilson, *A Pleasure Tree*
David Wojahn, *Glassworks*
David Wojahn, *Late Empire*
David Wojahn, *Mystery Train*
Paul Zimmer, *Family Reunion: Selected and New Poems*